THE PLATFORMIST

For permission to reprint more than several lines
of this book or for other inquiry, please write to
THE CULTURAL SOCIETY
culturalsociety.org | publisher@culturalsociety.org

Design by Zach Barocas
Cover photograph by Karl Gartung

Thanks to Cynthia Gray, Timothy Yu, Polly Morris, and John Tipton.

Some of these poems were previously printed in the following chapbooks
and print objects: *A Maximal Object* (Mitzvah Chaps), *Flags and Banners*
(Bronze Skull Press), *Precious* (Answer Tag Home Press), and
Asterisk (Number 13, Fewer & Further Press).

Thanks to Robert J. Baumann, Marie Larson,
Roberto Harrison, David Pavelich, and Jess Mynes
for their caring design and editorial work.

"Millions Now Living Will Never Die" was previously printed
as a broadside by Woodland Pattern Book Center.

Jay Millar and Mark Truscott printed "Precious" in its entirety in *BafterC*.

"Frisco Seal" was written for Stacy Szymaszek and published by her in *Gam*.

"The Aspiration Gene" was written for Dana Ward.
The poem first appeared in *Magazine Cypress*.

Certain of these poems found their first form in *The Cultural Society*, *Moria*,
Kulture Vulture, *Rust Buckle*, *Milk Magazine*, *Hutt*, *Kadar Koli*, *Work*,
Cannot Exist, *Moonlit*, and *Mrs. Maybe*.

Grateful acknowledgment to Zach Barocas, William Allegrezza, Justin Lacour,
Dustin Williamson, Larry Sawyer, Lina ramona Vitkauskas, Paul Hardacre,
David Hadbawnik, Roger Snell, David Harrison Horton, Andy Gricevich,
Lisa Janssen, Lauren Levin, Catherine Meng, and Jared Stanley.

All of my love and thanks, as always, to Cathy Cunningham.

THE PLATFORMIST
POEMS BY CHUCK STEBELTON

THE CULTURAL SOCIETY
BROOKLYN MMXII

CONTENTS

1   Millions Now Living Will Never Die

2   Cold Marble

3   Flags and Banners

4   Osage Orange

5   Endure

6   Talking Book

8   Must Utopia

9   Killdeer

10   Solus

11   After Clarence Ashley

12   The Heron (in Just-
     Spring)

14   A Phosphor

15   Toluene Summer

16   Crater Bar

17   Which Arrondissement

18   Natal Plum

19   G_d-forsaken Computer

20   Longing Repeatedly Fulfilled

21   Minus Nineteen Seconds

22   Longing Repeatedly Fulfilled

23   The Fourth Great Lake

24   New Saigon

25   Red Walls

26   Surround

27   Sixes and Sevens

28   Valentine

29   Frisco Seal

34   A Piney Ohio Is Inopportune

36   Green Grapes on Film

37   Under Wyoming

41   *Mnemosyne Creek*

43   *Precious*

58   *A Delay*

59   *A Second Delay*

60   *Futures*

61   *Factory*

62   *A Panic*

63   *The Aspiration Gene*

MILLIONS NOW LIVING WILL NEVER DIE

Sparking in every pattern likens silver to episodes.
Quieter starlings outnumber the sandpaper one.

Breezes swear you put Ohio in my impromptu.
Our ceiling fan praised leaves, and praises.

Heterogeneous icons. City hymnology

Giving grease a ride, an added scent enriched.
Down anthracite. He was my lover's maze.

Flora and fire went to Nevada to enjoy the laws.
Happiness increases as the population explodes.

If pubes be wool, wool wires bleat white.

Millions now living will never die. The calm could
be read once in a sitting and that sit was its allure.

COLD MARBLE

after Sherwood Anderson

One strategic wish

Pressed again. And all the bluebirds of happiness soaked. And delft.

The spidery boy and our dusty older brother. Orbit round his aerated head.

Now my old city sees me pick my burden up.

Salvo pressed against

Syllogism and the

Perfect world.

FLAGS AND BANNERS

The crowd upon their rambling exercise

And their feet were straight feet

and the sole of their feet was like

the sole of a calf's foot; and they sparkled

like the copper of burnished brass.

And they had the hands of a man under

their wings on their

four sides, and they four had their faces

and their wings. Their wings were joined

to another corrective;

they turned not when they went, then went

every one straight forward.

OSAGE ORANGE

Virulently anti-
prepositional
between the shady houses

of a pear tree, loaded
with suet and meshed.

The alimentary young elms

and a green plum tree
pared the white vinyl siding.

Rising easterly, mulberry
(earwigs there)
also the pussy willow,
as we called it,

and eggs under glass
(couple dozen)
perennially, so soon

to witness an Osage orange

between a handful
standing in as hedge apples
around the belly state.

Check all
emerald ash born
to chalk stone
for the plantings
in case a crystal text
itself were precedent.

ENDURE

There is another
lure. All visible

strength is threatening
to endure

Bad history
becomes pinched

While the scale
specifies

We shall be refined

As posited noise

TALKING BOOK

These walks wear
and these green

hills christen.

The robin
on the turret

and the Fulton
tear down on our path.

Cognates mash
in the affirmative.

The hurdles of
that nervousness end.

The acme novelties

state fictions
for everyone else.

§

So like
Eli to make
a talking
book
look bad.

§

Persimmons shook
often

once we stopped
to knock our weapons.

Still the peripheral

Lets an ideogram be.

MUST UTOPIA

"And without." LZ

Must utopia
Fall it is fall when
Is it alive here leaves turn
In alive as one stands
In time has suddenly as is
The fall.

Fall it is fall when
Is it alive leaves turn
In alive as stands
In time has suddenly as is
A fall. Must utopia.

KILLDEER

The grasses hinge on

a pencil pulled in two.

A dew claw in the grass.

Splintering skills

vestigial for a wing-bone.

SOLUS

Intrepid then, now

a throb rattles the trunk

      as circular thought
interrupts the impulse to jot it all down.

Body work sealed, blown clear
by a drier
blue exhaust.

AFTER CLARENCE ASHLEY

Above the drone

the thumb string drones
a cabinet clock

THE HERON (IN JUST-SPRING)

Meaty forays,

tangled forums

felt in the blue,

felt along the white.

Native born

in edible spring

a pattern is real.

§

Monadnock

and Rookery

might insist
on a single lens.

The heron flew east, the heron flew west,
She bare her over the fair forest.

A rustle
in the grass

is just the wind.

A pattern is real.

§

No black helicopters

on today

far and wheeling.

The balloon man
turns a silver oyster

into a twisted heron.

An agent is real.

A PHOSPHOR
for Peter O'Leary

I am the infinitesimal
world's dissimilar twin.

Sidereal

the winter wren.

Describe the beaks
with light on them.

Green, black, indigo

violet oscillation.

TOLUENE SUMMER

Teal dulls
the subtleties.

The coral
white heat

too close
to stereo

so court
and sparked

blue milk
crate diadems.

§

Xiphoid

Process is puddle

Slipping

§

Chrome trim
     held imitation

     Scotch pine,
          pin oak

A canopy
     thinning
          the vivid thing.

CRATER BAR

Amperes and the rare as a likely Puritan.

My green coffee cherries. Your improbable shoes.

Without wishful thinking we'd be enemies.

Water passed through the way a magnet pulls
through. This time that god was anxiety.

Hidden in the kitchen with His animals.

This is the splashy life based on factual spray.

WHICH ARRONDISSEMENT

We're here. We're unclear. Hang out the stars

in Anabasis. Between thirsty and frosty

Daffodils, half asparagus. Half public,

the forest on Indiana springs forward.

Weren't we there to expend slow pictures.

Utopia bent on the small catch and pheasants

in the field. If heaven began as property.

Left in the long grasses of Terre Haute

Enchainment, enchainment and plenitude.

An attitude so complete it never knew it.

NATAL PLUM

This myth proposes that it cast itself properly.

Ferns can chain link a fence in the snow.

My charmed try resulted in hope, again.
Last time I walk back down Metropolitan.

The revenant dreams a dream of history.

Blossom will little hummingbird. Collect

single gloves in the spirit of countless stars.

Monday, a nickel; Tuesday, a spoon.

Immolation is serial, hence its visibility.

Kiarostami says I tell little lies. Green hills,
cold, fold ruminants in their peaceable dream.

Natal Plum, Blue Rug or Wilton Carpet Juniper.

Flowering Quince, and Afghan Ash instanter.

G_D-FORSAKEN COMPUTER

That the Greeks chose not to name

tiny. Anaheim therein

involves woof. Equal pulses of breath

Frets upon the porky pine.

In my vicinity, survival intrigued

the curious. Salt in annals

Ending in stops. It is its own insult.

Take up thy Thucydides and walk.

A navy vying and an army vying.

I've held to the middle of a crooked tip.

LONGING REPEATEDLY FULFILLED

A hand like the sea, Antarctica.

Black hose at the gas station. Cold
metal, and blue and white vaseline.

The hemlocks heavy with feathers,

I dressed up in my flannel suit.
The aspen on their long parades.

Sandy and self regulatory
features defeat all sorts of looking.

A nickel to extend peculiar spoons.

MINUS NINETEEN SECONDS

Some of the former, a few of the latter staff.

Broadcast technology can afford this task once

hoops down the hallway and cotton balls soak

great red winter birds.

When evening pulls the ceiling
tight minus nineteen seconds.

Say you taped me. Ace this emerald verity.

We have cast wave technology. Notes on the cold

floor the pool of the spring. Nymph cases cotton

run slowworm and "high llamas" satellite.

A pantheon of hose
in your arterial tree.

She split the heel of she hand. Nature

is pedifem. Pace the glass surface of the sea.

LONGING REPEATEDLY FULFILLED

I got dressed up in my looking suit.

Ashes of credentials. Beeches

shift right, then down.

Longing repeatedly fulfilled.

The weather wants action.

Centered on film, grey shift. North

of everything eternally greening

the spread circles concentric.

THE FOURTH GREAT LAKE

"I love it here in bee effigies," yipped
Astro. The nets are golden in their sea.
"I piss upon the dehydrated cups."

Hands mar a certain fortitude. Some
liquors restore. In the band saw store
no one had too much to say.

A thistle in the beer, the flies are
out of work. There is no news in Deseret.

To respond requires a word on jewels.
Hands that have built the livery prone.
Hung in the scales with "Hum with."

NEW SAIGON

Bottom has
a synopsis.

Carping on

each hole and ache

so on indicator
panel pink

§

That white
superstructure

...which,..."which,"

ambiguous swallow

Halts the high

alerts

§

Lantern and tiled

incandescent
on Argyle.

Tony paper

(his New Saigon)

ash in the Tab can
infuriating

RED WALLS

Another spoon
bender in the lobby.

The net of next
events is thrown
wide to each.

The ordinal fireworks

and the cumulous
cloud as lead

floats and
leaf sinks.

SURROUND

Those punctual crows
and we have a hard time
drinking ice.

The ravenous grackle
and the earless
starling.

Limon tree
was sung. Becomes

elastic with oaks around.

SIXES AND SEVENS

All the people's
eyes locked
on Serena.

Sixes
and sevens
star. This art
is an only racket.

VALENTINE

Don't suffer it

As long as the plot thickens.

A numerical weed

Sunday or spill night

as lettuce in a gale.

Improbable dove

Unlikely in the straw

An apple bobbing

for euphemism

FRISCO SEAL

Tangram roofs in canopy light expose a charm that cannot be defined. It would be like speaking an unknown language to try to explain what brings me here.

If you have never felt that lure yourself, or if you think of it as a rare kind of bright room to visit after an evening's drinking, in a gang and for a lark.

The backslash and the solidus. The virgules are enjambed.
The humorless flower and the pulsating light.

This generational tenuousness.
Calls a cattail glass.

Hemorrhaging talent,

Nashville skyline is olfactory to me.

The pansy subtly alludes to fond memories.

The sinuous eskers and the tumbled

Norway spruce. This is a view of the seals. Tick season under an isosceles

Wax straps a floodlight in plastic sheeting late into the afternoon.

The same warns an orchard at night. Wool sounds fuzz boxed and clarity.

Since we sank back to the floor and called to the ground, "Show me static."

There is a windmill at the other end of the park, and a music mechanism.

Mucca
Pazza. Medium
Cool. Grass whistle
Or cut lip.

Pushbroom in the much loud

"Horizon" opened last night.

These dander birds and their histamines. Another question about the atom.

The decapitated and yet the stocking feet. The newest anchor. This the view

from the silverless.

If any accident of exposure is prescient. Primer lines

"Mash the cobalt

and carnelian of

that bird."

The floor that takes in the walls,

the stair, and the window.

If affinities

reappear. Black horse and the cherry

tree from the clavicle to St. Boniface.

Little lambs eat mâche at Budland.

Cattails

Haptic

when fashion
has thickened the skin.

To be unintended at the forks. Secure

a safe space for addressee. Now comes

love, the lazy.

                                        The "justifacatory"

obligates. It has no acoustical features.

Touch the spot of touch as

                        Heisman stance in full flannel survives a frisking,

hence the sect at his side.

Tinsel in the gum,

long may you burn. The ocean that won continues its spin.

Spell check humerus bone. On ice

I walked from the shuttle to the Strand.

Tehran splices into the move I'm making, emotional.

Now there are tones encircling me, which I understand means there is also a foil.

The embossing seal and the stunned wingers succumb.

A PINEY OHIO IS INOPPORTUNE

And if you wait another day, I will wait another day.

And if you wait another day, I will wait a day.

And the owl and the bat, neither one of them a bird.

And there is the collective hair. Centuries end

And the silvered stratus in the sudden twilight

And turns turn to black. A stream of smoke

And you will go out on your own. Idling

And revving will pass Lisa her White Shoulders.

And either the most progressive do not return.

And the simple boy lives in Hell. Tornados

And faster sections of the river know sand.

And better cinematographers know wood.

And the circadian clock entrains Virginia rails.

And Baltimore invests in its daily legend.

And here they remember how clearly color

And belts can turn. The two of you turn blue.

And if you wait another day, I will wait a day.

And if you wait another day, I will wait a day.

And I hate the cunning mantis, lean mimetic.

And the story repeats. And snow covers muck.

And the lotion begins to gild lemon grass.

And here white towels butter a collective hair.

And there are varieties in the corn. There mythical

And hungry streaks in the feline planks of barns

And lofty horrifics and rope ferment. White torino

And cobra rose farms thrive. Ampersand thorns

And hips trap teachers who die by their own hand.

And in that one room my father met his mechanic.

And an epic precedence of detail storms the silo.

And grapeshot scatters the genes. And epitaphs

And versatile fictions pass on the ultimate.

And a grain can be both politic and rooted.

And the circadian clock entrains another owl.

An arbutus grows at the edges of pine woods.

GREEN GRAPES ON FILM

The infant has an aftermath. Warm

clear

oil in the molasses cup.

Shellfish loaded, cocked for bear

take care great

blue.

The suffix sees Norfolk.

Smoke

goes sideways into "light and opacity."

UNDER WYOMING

Burned scale   boiler

Ohio Blue Tip

        pencil smell irises

Beyond the oil fire so

Wyoming is through.

A shell, a panic slight

Enough to wake slowly

Minnie Riperton's

Turn, fit only for

Easter pale blue.

§

A van full of tulips
moves through Akron.

Shoeboxes accumulate.

Dry leaves the elm little.

§

We pictured Eisenhower on the x-way.

Pharmaceuticals bloom.

§

On the seventh day of March
in a Polaroid year

A lucky epoch stuck nostalgia

For that rattling honk

The sour impulse of a tentative spleen

Very Superior Old Pale

Dry scent of printing.

§

The circular structure

video imposes

on a bridge on film.

Decades of taxis

between Wyoming

and its weather

§

after Kidlat Tahimik

Ornamental

the butt of a gun

breathed into

astronaut gin

dizzy smell

of jaundice

and hot dogs.

An aluminum

horse slick

with humidity

§

Weather films

"And rolls through,"

Ordinary

as a face forced into prayer.

Drawn

down. Tripling

perfume.

MNEMOSYNE CREEK

Numbers speak truth to poison.

Net or neo

Epistrophy

both sets

§

Sphere

brilliant corners

wink of forty

centuries

§

"And the Fjords

and the Aegean

are remembered."

§

Coit

counter windowpane

avenging

an occupation

§

Sedna has an eccentric

orbit.

Sedna was miserable.

No warmth in words.

PRECIOUS

I.

i

By this time tomorrow I will be a man of Xenia.

ii

Big
apostrophe

Don't we
want
to
fall like
leaves

iii

I come to revise Ohio, not to blame him.

Laconic, yes.

iv

I would rather not jump in front of our minutes.

v

A twelfth of an hour

vi

make cattle break their necks.

II

i

A commentary snapshot of the processes

ii

casements keep wet to themselves.

iii

Six hundred base six and you

iv

will know us by the trail of ants.

v

"black psalter"

vi

His was thirsty and sober. His epistema
follows the swell that made all things.

III

i

Brevity's lure,

ii

tells them until then. They've gone native
in the West's most participatory study.

iii

The varied topoi of obduracy fashions.

iv

Appeals to parting types fall on eyes.

v

Turtles hop past you. We knock
each other over like a minute hand

vi

baits a tiny hook.

IV

i

Precious,

ii

our bikes antiqued the city

iii

boats. Modal

iv

to sea in a sieve, sec-

v

ond star on the right

vi

and straight on till morning.

v

i

You're a flaneur in your aspiring flats

ii

and sloths in the attic. Toys

iii

land and Konyen last as song.
Nostalgia for the wall heroes reigns.

iv

I'm finna equate gonna here.

v

Internal conflict inside or outside the park

vi

to walk the city according to plan.

A DELAY

Willow oak, pin oak,
Swamp willow oak.
Swamp oak, water oak,
Spanish oak. Two oaks in all.

A SECOND DELAY

A swallowtail pivots.
Water oak, Spanish oak,
A pin oak static
In the pivotal grass.

FUTURES

Paper wings
might have wound

the tangling brushfoot

past fissures

FACTORY

The boredoms meet

Styx. We stole
the Saab you owned.

Because

clasp of a bracelet

equals

interest in Eric Gill

vocalists wrote 1864

for Antler

A PANIC

for Simon Pettet

Appropriate
Withnail and the lyrical
writ, decree

Appropriate
Withnail and the lyrical
writ, decree.

THE ASPIRATION GENE

I divorced my own orchid. His pitting core

is a just entendre. Nets in his soup

recall a colonial forest. The nativist trees

knotted direction, diversion. Aspiration

thought it meet. Winds in the exhale

thin like reeds. A dais for piney tops

to stay the accent gene. Project

object. This the age of fluorescents

proceeds along two tracks for four feet.

One winged herein, the other binocked.

As species, bison in the stars match

the solvent law within me. Ladder

bearable in the firmament match, tiny

hooves run a little vivid. Former

seconds of the alphabet, cyan thirds

address a heightened genetic. Ojai

put away its worldly music as such.

We sealed ours last year. First sight

at the isthmus "doubter." Wood decal

in the heat. Soft aspirated

cypher, a snow buries my wind rodeo.

Every accent done and felt. The very

latter especially. We met long enough

into the morning to account for Easter.

Horse mustache, a leech milking. "Asiatic

tradition," stressed the bobbed Atticist.

Attic style retained the spark of asterisk fire.

Intimacy and threat would continue to mix.

The complete fourth season on another island.

Pale best by southeast. The buffalo

suppose. In forensic silence in particular

a complex fear of lilts survives. Fared

primitive, more spare and wooden.

White pews erode the cliff. Ecstatic

calves land there composed of film and snow.

And we lived one house down. Neutrality

increasingly came to be seen as provocation.

Gone the beachcomber. Boxwood rats

eat pumpkin, slowly into carveable

pieces. The pipeline leans left of aisle.

The sons of the never wrong. It skips

a generation. Yesterday and today.

Man hands has rowdy feet. My lord

has hands like chairs. An animal's face

is a singular thing. Coal going

green in the fall into darkness, gone.

Comets freeze and Leonids fly.

Older timber to new. Boughs woven

with a motto put a hot straw under amber.

Two hours of Deuteronomy, half a day

to react and protect. Warm leatherette.

The dispassionate accent is its own trope.

The Welsh are less into Shinto. A waspy

cat hisses in the sorghum as waspy

cats hiss in the sorghum. The smuggest

grey Calumet, a part of a Northern cult.

Dig for ice. The rice is going to burn.

And feel the city air rush past uncut

with loops forming the pile. Quartets

hunt the plains. They violate the gunner

palace. Birder deep in the reply caches

blonde on electric heroics. Heroic

exits open on the right automatically.

Pro sabine tributes after a varietal can

frequent essential knowledge for doth.

It is therefore impossible to adopt a steer.

The wait results in belonging to tundra.

Oxidation is hilarious. An ornamental

cusp arcs. Still stars run on shift. Ton

voltage ramps up daisy rivers. Hellion

women sit out this pictorial set in riots.

We won one zero. A celebratory stroll

through the myrtle and the switches.

Will he still be blind or does he smell.

The peregrination gain cures hawks.

"His" money goes to war. Two to one

planetarians work in sister institutions.

Water and human habitations soften sleep.

Eminent men went oilily to the outlet store.

The "borrow our tribute to blunt intent."

Graphite is everywhere, its mines a continuum.

And green coal is a continuum of earth.

Each event returns us to quadratic weather.

Yet tar collapses. We too, closed to the will

to disperse. Imagine an attic room at an inn.

The panopoly now excludes a fire trick

with naptha, a tiny orange "bird" called

dikairon. Stymphalean birds pull elk.

Cloven plastic ovals hover, onion green.

Every hundred turned to copper in the field.

Noble because a shout in the surround

sound breaks or halts syndetic hearts.

The last retinal floater, a little appliance

problem. Carbon copies will not be read.

A winded meadow long on holdover

springs new cover and mechanical

obstruction. Hyperglossia cornered

a bagua, a field ordered by mending kit.

Chipped and vogueing on the linoleum

hung by a length of real human hair.

To prick the sides of my intent, but only

remotely like sonic compote besides

his faculties so meek. Thrift and lack

split a bird's tongue, a gram left in aspic.

A dozen loads in the drier on the eqinox.

Such is the case with Monday's wattage.

The pilot blew out with our last anthem.

Let us let who roll. But give me your gravity

in the red sea air, an airline of Eritrea.

This all you could drag. After so much

verbiage, we cross tangents, too. Dented

pewter. Forms which were arguably

more predictive. A conversation is said

to have been used to. Asia were

the shadow of yes. And we held a plurality.

All the ambition a breath can muster

makes new hours with solicitude.

Nets and gins are not set for poor birds.

Duplex, duplex! How fine that cry would be

at the movies. At the long depth of our talent

hemorrhage spirit. Telemarketers to enforce

yields of glass apple and lemon. A shift

before the populace. The Nixon era pandas

know where the summer goes when you're

under the gun. Our kitchen looks like hell.

Sings the silicone again. It's a deadpan

bet on the side of the loaded. Heads both

driving under par. With chipped feet

balled from the weather and the elephant

stone. His bowl anticipates a birdie.

Ye at the daubs flung up on they walls.

Wrinkle, leave me alone and sliver Sharon.

Rain is chief among the basket currencies.

A managed float stirs stratagem for refining

a channel for absorption. The cold frailties

and the heartening rivers. Traffic always

succumbs. This train is bound. Slowest

boat to the antipodes. Helium through glue.

The trefoil can testament a crescent moon.

The Seventeenth Century which moved

by consonants. Stares make scare quotes

scarce. An autumnal nose on a Sunday

afternoon. They precede us organically.

Points map a Dane's clarity. Intuition marks

those who wrote about techno, the most

nocturnal of all. Detroit swims into his ken.

Too hot to move. Your genome has appeal.

Along the human armament channel trained.

A stellar sea. Tip the bed to thin the beauty.

A ruminant with thighs which takes

the autological for granted. Dugonidae

blossom. A curriculum in wineskin. Venison

to be born. Raised as a seasonal

in the light of paramecium. Feet on the lotus

seen as the seeds of relativity. We were

there in the maps. One aspires to the shore.

Those who hoped to coax the remainder.

The flood came up and the indexes switched.

High over our pond the frail snap of a string.

Order a breathy request. A tone too deep

for peacocks. Twelve minutes with an insect

in my hand, being your vatic bird of paradise.

Hidden in a narrow vase. Pink is blue rhetoric

for fornication. Rigor plays out in the fields.

Pain in movement or whips these period.

Stuck branches sit and watch poise turn

to fig. We hated to internalize the heights.

Chuck Stebelton lives in Milwaukee, WI.
This is his second full-length collection of poetry.

§

THE PLATFORMIST

WAS PRINTED IN AN EDITION OF 250 COPIES
BY MCNAUGHTON & GUNN